Building Beyond Boundaries

The Remote-First Playbook for Entrepreneurial Success

Jesse S. Catoe

Copyright

All rights reserved. This book, including all text, illustrations, and other materials, is protected by copyright and international intellectual property laws. No part of this book may be reproduced, distributed, transmitted, or otherwise exploited in any form or by any means, without the prior written permission of the author.

Copyright © 2024 **Jesse S. Catoe**

First Edition: January 2024

Disclaimer

The information contained in this book is for informational purposes only and should not be construed as professional advice. The author disclaims any liability for any harm or damage arising from the use of the information contained herein.

Please respect the author's work and obtain proper permission before using any material from this book.

TABLE OF CONTENTS

Overview

The world of work has undergone a dramatic shift. Gone are the days of being tied to a physical office, confined by geography and traditional structures. Today, the rise of technology and a growing desire for flexibility and freedom has given birth to a new paradigm: the remote-first business model.

Building Beyond Boundaries is your comprehensive guide to navigating this exciting frontier. This book is designed to empower entrepreneurs like you to build and manage successful businesses with geographically dispersed teams. Whether you're a seasoned entrepreneur or just starting, this book provides you with the essential knowledge, tools, and strategies you need to thrive in the remote-first world.

What you will learn:

- The compelling case for remote-first: Discover the numerous benefits of the remote-first model, from increased talent pool and reduced overhead to improved employee engagement and productivity.

- Building a high-performing remote team: Learn how to attract, hire, onboard, and manage top talent in a remote environment. We'll cover everything from fostering a culture of trust and transparency to building strong relationships and facilitating effective communication.

- Mastering the remote workflow: Explore the latest tools and technologies that can help your team collaborate seamlessly, regardless of location. We'll delve into project management software, communication platforms, and tools for asynchronous collaboration.

- Scaling your remote-first business: Learn how to develop a scalable infrastructure that can support your growth. We'll cover topics such as remote team leadership, building a remote-friendly culture, and overcoming common challenges.

- The future of remote work: Get a glimpse into the exciting possibilities that lie ahead for remote-first businesses. We'll explore emerging trends, discuss the future of work, and equip you with the knowledge you need to stay ahead of the curve.

This book is for you if:

- You are an entrepreneur who is considering starting or transitioning to a remote-first business.
- You are a leader of a team that is partially or fully remote.
- You are interested in learning more about the benefits and challenges of the remote-first model.
- You are looking for practical advice and strategies for building a successful remote team.
- You are curious about the future of work and how it will impact the way we do business.

Part 1: Foundations of Remote-First Success

Introduction

A Paradigm Shift in the World of Work

The landscape of labor is enduring a dramatic metamorphosis. The days of being chained to a physical office, confined by geography and traditional structures, are swiftly vanishing into the rearview mirror. In their stead, a new paradigm is emerging, fuelled by the convergence of technological advancements and a growing desire for flexibility and freedom: the remote-first business model.

This transition is not a novelty, but a fundamental transformation in the way we work and collaborate. Driven by the rise of cloud computing, collaboration tools, and high-speed internet, remote work is no longer an aberration, but an increasingly mainstream reality. According to a recent study by FlexJobs, 57% of employees now work remotely at least once a week, with that figure expected to rise in the future years.

But why are businesses embracing remote-first models in droves? The answer resides in the multiplicity of benefits they offer, including:

Access to a global talent pool: Businesses are no longer limited to recruiting within their geographical area. They can now delve into a vast reservoir of talented individuals from around the globe, regardless of their location.

Reduced overhead: Remote work eliminates the need for costly office space and associated costs, resulting in significant savings for businesses.

Improved employee engagement and productivity: Studies have shown that remote workers often report higher levels of satisfaction, engagement, and productivity compared to their office-based counterparts.

Increased agility and flexibility: Remote-first businesses are better suited to adapt to changing market conditions and customer requirements due to their flexible and distributed nature.

Enhanced employee well-being: Remote work enables employees to achieve a better work-life balance by minimizing commuting time and offering greater flexibility in scheduling.

Of course, the transition to a remote-first model comes with its own set of challenges. Building trust, nurturing collaboration, and maintaining a strong company culture can be more difficult in a geographically dispersed environment. However, with the proper strategies and tools in place, these challenges can be surmounted, paving the way for a thriving remote-first organization.

This book is your guide to navigating this thrilling new frontier. We will delve into the foundations of remote-first success, investigating the key principles, strategies, and best practices you need to know to establish and manage a successful remote team. We will equip you with the knowledge and resources to: Attract and retain top talent from around the globe.

Build a robust and cohesive remote culture.

Master asynchronous communication and collaboration.

Manage your remote team effectively and overcome common challenges.

Embrace the future of employment and create a sustainable and resilient business.

The journey to a successful remote-first enterprise is an exciting one, replete with challenges and opportunities. Let us embark on this voyage together and uncover the transformative power of remote work.

Chapter 1: The Remote Revolution: Why Now is the Time for Remote-First Businesses

In 2012, a small software company named Zapier was founded with a bold vision: to create a remote-first workplace where talented individuals could work from anywhere in the world. This evidently radical idea was met with skepticism and doubt. Many questioned the feasibility of administering a geographically dispersed workforce and whether it could foster essential collaboration and innovation.

Fast forward to today, and Zapier stands as a testament to the success of the remote-first model. With over 400 employees dispersed across 30 countries, the company has achieved remarkable growth and profitability. Their tale is not unique. From global titans like Automattic and GitLab to innumerable startups and small businesses, organizations of all sizes are embracing the remote-first model and reaping its benefits.

This unprecedented growth can be attributed to several important factors

1. Technological Advancements: The rise of cloud computing, collaboration tools like Slack and Zoom, and high-speed internet has removed the technological barriers that once hindered remote work. Today, teams can seamlessly collaborate and exchange information regardless of their location, making remote work a viable option for virtually any industry.

2. **Evolving Work Landscape:** The conventional office-based model is no longer the sole driver of success. In an era of globalization and rapid technological change, businesses need to be agile and adaptable. Remote-first models offer greater flexibility and resilience, allowing organizations to rapidly scale up or down based on market requirements.

3. Changing Workforce Preferences: The modern workforce is increasingly demanding flexibility and autonomy. Millennials and Gen Z, in particular, value work-life balance and the freedom to work from anywhere. Companies that embrace remote work can attract and retain top talent, giving them a competitive edge in the marketplace.

4. **A** Global Talent Pool: By eliminating geographical boundaries, remote-first enterprises can draw into a vast and diverse talent pool. This opens doors to expertise and skills that may not be readily available in their local market, leading to increased innovation and creativity.

5. Cost Savings: Remote work can contribute to significant cost reductions for enterprises. Eliminating the need for office space, utilities, and commuting expenditures can free up resources to be reinvested in other areas of the business, such as employee development and technology.

The Case of Zapier

Zapier's story provides a tangible example of the benefits of a remote-first model. The company has experienced rapid growth, attaining profitability in just three years and multiplying its revenue every year. This prosperity can be attributed to the following factors:

Focus on talent: Zapier prioritizes hiring the finest individuals, regardless of their location. They believe that a diverse and talented workforce is essential for innovation and success.

Building trust and transparency: Zapier fosters a culture of trust and transparency by over-communicating and encouraging open dialogue. This helps to develop strong relationships and ensures everyone feels connected and engaged.

Investing in technology: Zapier utilizes a variety of tools and technologies to facilitate collaboration and communication. This enables employees to operate effectively from anywhere in the world.

Empowering employees: Zapier gives employees a high degree of autonomy and encourages them to take ownership of their work. This fosters a sense of responsibility and motivation, leading to increased productivity and engagement.

The success of Zapier and innumerable other remote-first enterprises is unmistakable evidence that the remote revolution is well underway. As technology continues to evolve and the workforce demands greater flexibility, we can expect to see more and more businesses adopt this innovative model.

Chapter 2: The Remote-First Mindset: Embracing a New Way of Working

Transitioning to a remote-first model requires more than just technology and tools. It demands a fundamental shift in mindset and a deep understanding of the principles that underpin a successful remote-first organization. At its core, the remote-first mindset is built on three pillars:

1. Trust: The cornerstone of any successful remote team is trust. Leaders must trust their employees to be productive and responsible, regardless of their location. This trust empowers employees to work independently and make decisions without constant oversight.

Studies show that employees who feel trusted are more engaged, productive, and satisfied with their jobs. A survey by Buffer revealed that 84% of remote workers believe that trust is the most important factor in a positive remote work experience.

Building Trust in a Remote Environment

Set clear expectations and goals: Clearly define what success looks like for each role and project.

Empower employees with the resources and autonomy they need to succeed.

Communicate openly and honestly, both positive and the negative feedback.

Promote transparency in decision-making processes.

Recognize and reward achievements.

2. Transparency: Open and transparent communication is essential for fostering trust and collaboration in a remote environment. Leaders must be open and honest about company goals, challenges, and decisions. Employees need access

to information and updates to feel informed and connected.

A study by McKinsey found that companies with high levels of transparency experience higher levels of employee engagement, innovation, and decision-making speed.

Enhancing Transparency in a Remote Setting

Hold regular team meetings and company-wide updates.

Share documents and information openly.

Encourage open communication and feedback.

Utilize tools and platforms that facilitate information sharing.

Lead by example by being frank and transparent.

3. Autonomy: Remote work offers a unique opportunity to empower employees with autonomy

and ownership over their work. By giving employees the freedom to manage their time and schedule, businesses can unlock their full potential and drive innovation.

Research by Harvard Business Review showed that employees who have greater autonomy experience increased creativity, productivity, and job satisfaction.

Empowering Employees in a Remote Environment

Set clear goals and objectives, but allow employees the freedom to choose how to achieve them.

Provide employees with regular feedback and coaching.

Create a culture of experimentation and learning.

Celebrate successes and encourage risk-taking.

Support professional development opportunities.

The Benefits of a Flexible Work Environment

Embracing a remote-first mindset and implementing flexible work arrangements offer numerous benefits for both employees and employers:

For Employees

Improved work-life balance and reduced stress.

Increased flexibility and control over work schedule.

Reduced commuting time and associated costs.

Greater autonomy and ownership over work.

Improved job satisfaction and engagement.

For Employers

Access to a wider talent pool.

Reduced overhead costs associated with office space.

Increased employee retention and engagement.

Improved productivity and innovation.

Greater agility and responsiveness to market changes.

Case Study: Buffer

Buffer, a social media management platform, has been a pioneer in the remote-first movement. Since its founding in 2010, the company has operated solely with a remote team. Buffer's commitment to transparency and autonomy has attracted top talent and fostered a culture of innovation. The company has experienced significant growth and boasts a highly engaged team with a 90% satisfaction rate.

NB:Shifting to a remote-first mindset requires a conscious effort and a commitment to building trust, transparency, and autonomy. By embracing these principles and implementing flexible work arrangements, businesses can unlock a world of benefits for both employees and employers.

Chapter 3: Building a High-Performing Remote Team: Talent Acquisition, Onboarding, and Management Strategies

In the vibrant landscape of remote work, attracting and retaining top talent is crucial for creating a high-performing team. This chapter will equip you with the essential strategies and best practices to navigate this terrain, paving the way for success in your remote-first organization.

Attracting the best:

Casting a broader net

Leverage online platforms like LinkedIn, Indeed, and AngelList to reach a global talent pool.

Partner with remote-specific employment platforms and communities.

Attend online conferences and events relevant to your industry.

Build relationships with universities and colleges with strong programs in your field.

Selling your remote-first advantage

Highlight the benefits of a flexible work environment, such as enhanced work-life balance and increased productivity.

Showcase your company culture and values through your website, social media, and employee testimonials.

Offer competitive compensation and benefits packages that accommodate remote workers.

Promote your commitment to professional development and growth opportunities.

Building a talent pipeline

Develop a robust employer brand that attracts top talent.

Implement a referral program to incentivize existing employees to recommend qualified candidates.

Create a talent pool of potential candidates for future openings.

Build relationships with potential candidates through social media and networking events.

Onboarding for success:

Creating a seamless transition

Establish a distinct and well-defined induction process.

Assign a dedicated mentor or companion to each new team member.

By provide access to all necessary resources and information.

Schedule regular check-ins and provide feedback.

Implement virtual team-building exercises to cultivate a sense of unity and cooperation.

Setting expectations

Communicate company goals, values, and expectations.

Assign duties and obligations to each member of the team.

Establish communication protocols and instruments.

Set performance metrics and provide regular feedback.

Offer opportunities for professional development and growth.

Building a sense of belonging: Introduce new team members virtually to the entire team.

Organize social events and virtual coffee breaks.

Encourage informal communication and interaction.

Create virtual communities and interest groups.

Celebrate milestones and achievements together.

Managing and motivating remote teams:

Building trust and facilitating communication

Over-communicate and be as transparent as feasible.

Promote frank dialogue.

Regularly solicit feedback from team members.

Provide opportune recognition and appreciation.

Utilize a variety of communication channels, including video conferencing, instant messaging, and project management tools.

Maintaining engagement and productivity

Set explicit objectives and expectations.

Empower the team members with autonomy and ownership over their work.

Provide opportunities for collaboration and innovation.

Offer flexible work schedules and arrangements.

Invest in technologies and tools that enable remote work.

Addressing prospective challenges

Combat isolation and loneliness by fostering a strong sense of community.

Implement strategies to address time zone differences and asynchronous communication.

Establish clear boundaries between professional and personal spheres.

Offer assistance and resources to promote mental and physical health.

Case Study: GitLab

GitLab, a leading software development platform, has effectively created a high-performing remote workforce of over 1,300 employees spread across 65 countries. Their success is attributed to their concentration on transparency, autonomy, and a strong remote culture. GitLab provides all employees with the resources and support they need to flourish in a remote environment, nurturing a sense of community and belonging.

Building a high-performing remote team requires a strategic approach that goes beyond simply recruiting talented individuals. By implementing effective talent acquisition strategies, constructing a seamless onboarding process, and employing best practices for managing and motivating your team, you can unleash the potential of your remote workforce and achieve remarkable success. As you embark on this voyage, remember to cultivate trust, communication, and a sense of belonging. This will establish the foundation for a thriving remote team that delivers exceptional results and propels your organization forward.

Part 2: Remote-First Operations: Systems and Processes for Efficiency and Collaboration

Chapter 4: The Remote-First Workflow: Tools and Technologies for Seamless Collaboration

In the dynamic world of remote work, seamless collaboration is the cornerstone of success. But how do you reconcile the geographical divide and ensure your team can work together effectively, regardless of location? The answer resides in the strategic implementation of the latest tools and technologies. This chapter will guide you through the extensive landscape of collaboration solutions, empowering you to unleash the full potential of your remote-first team.

Project Management Software: Orchestrating Success

Centralize tasks and projects: Tools like Asana, Trello, and Monday.com offer a centralized platform for designating tasks, monitoring progress, and collaborating on projects.

Simplify communication: Eliminate the need for interminable email threads by keeping all project-related information in one place.

Boost transparency: Everyone involved in the initiative has access to real-time updates and progress reports, fostering accountability and trust.

Streamline workflows: Automate repetitive duties and construct customizable workflows to optimize your team's efficiency.

Case Study

Automattic, the juggernaut behind WordPress, leverages Asana to manage projects and collaborate effectively across its geographically dispersed team of over 1,200 employees.

Communication Platforms: Bridging the Distance

Real-time connections: Video conferencing tools like Zoom, Google Meet, and Microsoft Teams enable seamless face-to-face communication, replicating the in-person experience.

Instant messaging: Platforms like Slack and Microsoft Teams provide a convenient method for fast communication, informal discussions, and brainstorming sessions.

File sharing and collaboration: Share documents, presentations, and other files effortlessly with tools like Dropbox, Google Drive, and OneDrive.

Global reach: These platforms offer features like international dialing and language translations, facilitating communication across time zones and cultures.

Case Study

Zapier, a leading automation platform, utilizes Slack as its primary communication center, nurturing a vibrant and connected remote culture.

Tools for Asynchronous Collaboration: Working Smarter, Not Harder

Embrace asynchronous communication: Tools like Notion, Coda, and Confluence enable for comprehensive documentation, note-taking, and real-time collaboration, even when team members are in different time zones.

Promote deep thinking: Asynchronous communication encourages thoughtful responses and reduces the strain of immediate replies, leading to more informed decisions.

Increase accessibility: Asynchronous tools make information readily available to all team members, regardless of their schedule or location.

Boost productivity: Asynchronous communication allows team members to work at their own tempo, maximizing their focus and productivity.

Case Study

GitLab, a software development platform, thrives on asynchronous collaboration. Their use of tools like GitLab Docs and Slack threads allows for in-depth discussions and facilitates knowledge sharing across the globe.

Constructing a Tech Stack That Suits Your Needs:

Identify your team's requirements and workflows.

Invest in tools that integrate seamlessly with each other.

Prioritize user-friendliness and simplicity of adoption.

Gather feedback and refine your tech platform continuously.

Beyond the Tools

Develop explicit communication guidelines and protocols.

Set expectations for availability and responsiveness.

Encourage frank and transparent communication.

Foster a culture of respect and understanding.

The proper tools and technologies can revolutionize the way your remote team collaborates. By selecting the right solutions, implementing them effectively, and nurturing a culture of collaboration, you can unleash unprecedented levels of productivity, creativity, and engagement. Remember, the true power resides not in the tools themselves, but in how you utilize them to empower your team to accomplish extraordinary results.

Chapter 5: Mastering Asynchronous Communication: Building Trust, Transparency, and Alignment

In the vibrant landscape of remote work, asynchronous communication reigns paramount. As the traditional office environment dissipates into the background, the ability to collaborate effectively across time zones and cultures becomes paramount. This chapter delves into the intricacies of asynchronous communication, empowering you with the tools and strategies to cultivate trust, transparency, and alignment in your remote team.

The Power of Asynchronous Communication

Time Zone Freedom: Asynchronous communication enables team members to work at their own tempo, regardless of location or schedule. This flexibility empowers individuals to maximize their productivity and contribute to initiatives at their optimum performance.

Deeper Thinking: By removing the burden of immediate responses, asynchronous communication encourages deliberate, well-considered contributions. This leads to more informed decision-making and a higher quality of discussion.

Increased Accessibility: Asynchronous tools like project management software, documentation platforms, and communication channels make information readily available to all team members, regardless of their schedule or location. This ensures everyone is on the same page and eliminates information silos.

Improved Transparency: Asynchronous communication creates a detailed record of discussions and decisions. This transparency fosters trust and accountability and allows for future reference and knowledge sharing.

Strategies for Effective Asynchronous Communication

Clearly articulate your thoughts and expectations.

Use concise and organized language.

Provide context and prior information for complex topics.

Use visuals and multimedia to enhance understanding.

Proofread and edit your messages attentively before transmitting them.

Set explicit deadlines and expectations for response periods.

Be mindful of cultural differences and communication patterns.

Encourage frank dialogue and ask clarifying questions.

Utilize tools and features that facilitate asynchronous collaboration.

Building Trust and Transparency

Establish explicit communication guidelines and protocols.

Be responsive and expeditious in your communication.

Provide regular updates and progress reports.

Acknowledge and appreciate contributions from team members.

Be open to feedback and willing to adapt your communication approach.

Overcoming Challenges

Language Barriers: Implementing language translation tools and fostering cultural sensitivity can facilitate cross-cultural communication.

Information Overload: Utilize distinct organization, structure, and searchable tools to manage information effectively.

Lack of Social Interaction: Promote virtual team-building activities and encourage informal communication channels to foster connection.

Case Study: Automattic

Automattic, the juggernaut behind WordPress, thrives on asynchronous communication. Their team utilizes a variety of tools, including Slack threads, email threads, and Notion documents, to collaborate effectively across time zones and cultures. This approach allows for profound pondering, knowledge sharing, and a high level of transparency within the organization.

Mastering asynchronous communication is not merely a matter of using the correct tools, but also about cultivating a culture of trust, transparency, and alignment. By embracing the power of asynchronous communication, you can empower your remote team to collaborate effectively, accomplish remarkable results, and unleash a world of possibilities. Remember, the key rests in clear communication, deliberate consideration, and a profound comprehension of your team's needs and preferences.

Chapter 6: Fostering a Culture of Connection: Building Strong Relationships in a Remote Environment

In the ever-evolving landscape of remote employment, the need for connection remains paramount. While the tangible office may be absent, the human desire for belonging and camaraderie persists. This chapter delves into the strategies and initiatives that can nurture strong relationships and create a thriving remote culture, where team members feel valued, connected, and empowered.

The Importance of Connection

Improved employee satisfaction and engagement: Studies show that strong relationships and a positive remote culture contribute to increased satisfaction, engagement, and reduced turnover.

Enhanced collaboration and innovation: When team members feel connected and supported, they are more likely to collaborate effectively, share ideas candidly, and drive innovation.

Boosted morale and well-being: A strong remote culture can mitigate feelings of isolation and loneliness, fostering mental well-being and resilience among team members.

Enhanced employer brand: Building a strong remote culture can attract and retain top talent, giving your company a competitive edge in the marketplace.

Strategies for Building Strong Relationships

Virtual team-building activities: Organize online games, quizzes, social events, and virtual coffee breaks to promote informal interaction and relationship building.

Mentorship programs: Pair experienced team members with recruits to provide guidance, support, and a sense of belonging.

Internal communication channels: Utilize tools like Slack channels, forums, and internal communication platforms to encourage open communication and knowledge sharing.

Regular check-ins and one-on-one meetings: Hold regular individual and team meetings to communicate on a personal level, discuss goals and progress, and provide feedback.

Celebrating successes and milestones: Acknowledge and celebrate individual and team achievements to bolster morale and cultivate a sense of collective accomplishment.

Fostering a Sense of Community

Create virtual communities and interest groups: Cater to diverse interests and encourage team members to communicate and share their passions outside of work.

Implement social recognition programs: Recognize and reward team members for their contributions, nurturing a sense of appreciation and belonging.

Encourage informal communication and interaction: Create opportunities for casual conversations and social interaction, such as virtual water cooler discussions and online game evenings.

Organize company-wide events and retreats: Bring the remote team together periodically for face-to-face interaction, collaboration, and team cohesion.

Promote transparency and open communication: Share company news, updates, and decisions candidly with the entire team to foster trust and inclusivity.

Case Study: Zapier

Zapier, a prominent automation platform, has cultivated a flourishing remote culture known for its strong sense of community. They prioritize regular team-building activities, facilitate informal communication, and recognize individual and team achievements. This investment in connection has resulted in a highly engaged workforce and a company culture that attracts top talent.

Building a strong remote culture requires intentional effort and a consistent commitment to nurturing connection. By implementing the strategies enumerated in this chapter, you can create a vibrant and inclusive environment where team members feel valued, supported, and empowered to flourish. Remember, the key is to be creative, intentional, and focused on developing genuine relationships that will inspire collaboration, innovation, and long-term success in your remote-first organization.

Part 3: Scaling Remote-First: Growth Strategies and Leadership Development

Chapter 7: Building a Scalable Remote Infrastructure: Creating a System that Supports Growth

As your remote-first business expands, it's crucial to ensure your infrastructure can adapt and develop seamlessly. This chapter delves into the essential elements of a scalable infrastructure, providing you with the tools and strategies to navigate the challenges of growth and establish a foundation for long-term success.

The Need for Scalability

Accommodating growth: A scalable infrastructure allows you to seamlessly add new team members, projects, and data without confronting system bottlenecks or performance issues.

Ensuring flexibility: It enables you to adapt to altering market conditions, technology trends, and new business opportunities.

Reducing costs: By optimizing resource utilization and avoiding superfluous investments in hardware and software, you can achieve significant cost savings.

Key Elements of a Scalable Remote Infrastructure

1. Cloud-based solutions: Leveraging cloud computing platforms like Amazon Web Services (AWS), Microsoft Azure, and Google Cloud Platform (GCP) offers flexibility, scalability, and global reach.

Cloud-based solutions simplify infrastructure management, reduce maintenance costs, and provide access to a broad selection of tools and services.

2. Secure data management: Implementing comprehensive data security measures is essential for safeguarding sensitive information and complying with industry regulations.

Utilize encryption technologies, access controls, and intrusion detection systems to safeguard sensitive data.

Develop explicit data governance policies and procedures to ensure responsible data handling.

3. Reliable IT infrastructure: Investing in reliable hardware, software, and network connectivity is essential for assuring optimal performance and availability.

Implement regular maintenance and monitoring procedures to identify and address potential issues before they impact business operations.

Establish redundancy plans and disaster recovery protocols to minimize disruption and ensure business continuity in unforeseen circumstances.

4. Automation and integration: Automating repetitive duties and workflows can improve efficiency, reduce errors, and open up employee time for more strategic work.

Integrate your communication, collaboration, and project management tools to create a seamless workflow and enhance collaboration.

Invest in robotic process automation (RPA) solutions to automate routine duties and enhance operational efficiency.

5. Continuous monitoring and improvement:

Regularly monitor your infrastructure performance and identify areas for improvement.

Gather feedback from team members and stakeholders to comprehend their requirements and pain points.

Proactively alter and evolve your infrastructure based on changing business requirements and technological advancements.

Case Study: Buffer, a social media administration platform, leverages a cloud-based infrastructure that scales seamlessly with its increasing user base. Their commitment to data security and reliable IT infrastructure ensures business continuity and protects sensitive user information.

Building a scalable remote infrastructure is an ongoing process that requires meticulous planning, continuous monitoring, and a commitment to innovation. By implementing the strategies enumerated in this chapter, you can create a foundation for sustainable growth and empower your remote-first business to flourish in the dynamic world of work. Remember, scalability is not just about technology, but also about establishing a flexible and adaptable organization that can embrace change and continuously evolve to meet future challenges and opportunities

Chapter 8: Leading Remote Teams: Strategies for Effective Communication, Motivation, and Feedback

Leading a remote team requires a refined set of skills and strategies distinct from the traditional office environment. This chapter delves into the unique challenges and opportunities of remote leadership, empowering you with the tools and techniques to effectively communicate, motivate, and provide feedback to your geographically dispersed team.

Challenges of Leading Remote Teams

Maintaining visibility and engagement: Without regular face-to-face interaction, it can be difficult to remain connected with team members and gauge their level of engagement.

Building trust and rapport: Establishing trust and rapport remotely requires a more deliberate effort, as informal interactions and social signals are often limited.

Providing precise and expeditious communication: Effective communication is crucial in any team environment, but it becomes even more important when team members are not physically present.

Managing cultural differences: Leading a diverse team with members from various cultures requires sensitivity and understanding to navigate communication patterns and work preferences.

Opportunities of Leading Remote Teams

Access to a broader talent pool: Remote work allows you to recruit top talent regardless of their location, expanding your access to a diverse pool of experienced individuals.

Increased flexibility and autonomy: Remote work can increase employee fulfillment and engagement by providing greater flexibility and control over work schedules and locations.

Improved communication skills: Effective remote leadership requires strong written and verbal communication skills, which can benefit both leaders and team members.

Reduced costs: A remote workforce can contribute to significant cost savings associated with office space, utilities, and commuting expenses.

Strategies for Effective Communication

Over-communicate: Be proactive in sharing information, updates, and decisions with your team.

Utilize various communication channels: Employ a blend of tools, including video conferencing, instant messaging, and project management platforms, to accommodate to different communication styles.

Set clear expectations and guidelines: Establish explicit communication protocols, define response times, and ensure everyone understands their role and responsibilities.

Practice active listening: Pay close attention to verbal and nonverbal cues, and encourage frank dialogue and feedback.

Be transparent and honest: Build trust by being transparent and honest in all communications, even when delivering difficult news.

Motivating and Providing Feedback to Remote Teams:

Set clear objectives and expectations: Define individual and team objectives, provide regular feedback, and celebrate achievements.

Offer opportunities for growth and development: Invest in training and development programs to help team members acquire new skills and advance their professions.

Recognize and reward contributions: Acknowledge and appreciate individual and team successes to enhance morale and motivation.

Provide regular and constructive feedback: Offer precise, actionable feedback to help team members enhance their performance.

Focus on strengths and areas for development: Celebrate strengths while providing specific and actionable feedback for improvement.

Use multiple methods for providing feedback: Utilize different methods, such as written feedback, one-on-one meetings, and peer-to-peer feedback, to accommodate to individual preferences.

Case Study: GitLab, a prominent software development platform, leverages asynchronous communication and a culture of transparency to effectively lead their remote team. Their focus on open dialogue, regular feedback, and explicit expectations has nurtured a highly motivated and engaged workforce.

Leading a remote team requires a unique set of skills and a commitment to establishing trust, transparency, and effective communication. By implementing the strategies enumerated in this chapter, you can cultivate a thriving remote culture where team members feel valued, engaged, and empowered to accomplish extraordinary results. Remember, effective remote leadership is not about micromanaging, but about creating a supportive and empowering environment that enables your team to flourish and contribute their best work, regardless of their location.

Chapter 9: Remote-First Leadership: Developing the Skills to Lead a Distributed Workforce

In the ever-evolving landscape of remote work, the function of the leader takes on a new dimension. Effective leadership in this environment requires a unique combination of skills and qualities that go beyond the traditional leadership model. This chapter delves into the essential characteristics of a successful remote-first leader, providing you with a roadmap for developing the competencies required to guide and empower your geographically dispersed team.

Essential Skills and Qualities of a Remote-First Leader

Strong communication: The ability to communicate explicitly, concisely, and effectively across various channels is paramount. Leaders must be adept at written and verbal communication, tailoring their approach to various audiences and situations.

Transparency and trust: Building trust with your team is essential for nurturing collaboration and engagement. Being transparent in your decisions, actions, and communication demonstrates openness and builds a foundation of trust.

Empathy and understanding: Recognizing and acknowledging the challenges and opportunities of remote work is crucial. Leaders should be empathetic to individual requirements and circumstances, creating a supportive and inclusive environment.

Delegation and empowerment: Micromanagement has no place in a remote-first environment. Effective leaders delegate tasks effectively, empower their team members to take ownership, and provide clear expectations and support.

Adaptability and flexibility: The ability to adjust to change and adopt new technologies is essential.

Leaders must be flexible in their approach and willing to modify their strategies based on evolving circumstances.

Vision and strategic thinking: Setting a clear vision for the future and devising effective strategies to attain that vision is crucial. Leaders must be able to communicate this vision effectively and inspire their team to move forward.

Mentorship and coaching: Providing guidance and support to team members is critical for their development and success. Leaders should be proficient at providing feedback, offering mentorship opportunities, and nurturing a culture of continuous learning.

Developing Remote-First Leadership Skills

Self-reflection: Regularly assess your strengths and weaknesses as a leader, identify areas for advancement, and set objectives for personal development.

Seek feedback: Actively solicit feedback from your team members, colleagues, and mentors to obtain valuable insights into your leadership style and identify areas for improvement.

Invest in training and development: Various resources, seminars, and programs can help you refine your leadership skills specific to leading remote teams.

Join professional communities and networks: Connecting with other remote-first leaders through online forums, conferences, or communities can provide valuable peer-to-peer learning and support.

Become a perpetual learner: Embrace the continuous learning spirit and remain updated on the latest trends, technologies, and best practices in remote leadership.

Case Study: Automattic, the juggernaut behind WordPress, prioritizes leadership development for its remote-first culture. They offer comprehensive training programs, mentoring opportunities, and leadership development initiatives that empower individuals to grow into effective remote leaders.

The journey to becoming an effective remote-first leader begins with self-awareness, a commitment to continuous learning, and a genuine desire to connect and empower your geographically dispersed team. By cultivating the essential skills and qualities enumerated in this chapter, you can navigate the challenges and opportunities of remote work, create a thriving remote culture, and lead your team to accomplish extraordinary results. Remember, remote-first leadership is a journey, not a destination. Embrace the process of perpetual growth and development, and you will be well-equipped to guide your team toward a future of success and fulfillment.

Part 4: The Remote-First Future: Opportunities and Challenges

Chapter 10: The Future of Work is Remote: Embracing the Potential of a Global Workforce

The world of work is enduring a seismic transition, with the landscape increasingly characterized by a remote workforce. This chapter delves into the exciting future of remote work, investigating the burgeoning potential of a globalized talent pool and the transformative impact of emergent technologies.

The Rise of the Remote Revolution

Unprecedented growth: Studies project that the global remote workforce will reach 1.8 billion by 2027, highlighting the exponential development of this work model.

Technological advancements: Cloud computing, collaboration tools, and virtual reality are paving the way for seamless remote work experiences, blurring the geographical boundaries of the workplace.

Shifting employee preferences: Millennials and Gen Z, who now represent a significant segment of the workforce, value flexibility, and work-life balance, driving the demand for remote work options.

Global talent pool: By embracing remote work, businesses gain access to a diverse and qualified talent pool from across the globe, unleashing a wealth of expertise and innovation.

Emerging Trends Shaping the Future

Artificial intelligence (AI): AI-powered tools will automate routine duties, freeing up human workers to focus on creativity, problem-solving, and strategic thinking.

Virtual reality (VR): VR technology will create immersive virtual workstations, facilitating collaboration and communication more engagingly and interactively.

The gig economy: The rise of the gig economy will offer individuals greater flexibility and autonomy, enabling them to work on projects and contracts that align with their talents and interests.

Decentralized work organizations (DAOs): DAOs will facilitate collaborative work without the need for a traditional hierarchical structure, fostering greater ownership and engagement among team members.

Opportunities for Businesses

Reduced costs: Lower administrative expenses associated with office space, utilities, and commuting can contribute to significant cost savings for businesses.

Enhanced talent acquisition: Access to a larger and more diverse talent pool can lead to recruiting top talent regardless of location.

Increased employee engagement and satisfaction: Remote work can offer greater flexibility, work-life harmony, and career autonomy, leading to happier and more engaged employees.

Improved agility and innovation: A global workforce can bring diverse perspectives and ideas to the table, fostering a more innovative and competitive organization.

Challenges to Address

Cybersecurity risks: Ensuring data security and protecting sensitive information requires robust cybersecurity measures and employee awareness.

Remote fatigue and burnout: Maintaining work-life balance and avoiding exhaustion in a remote environment requires intentional efforts and clear boundaries.

Cultural differences: Managing a diverse team across various cultures and time zones necessitates cultural sensitivity and effective communication strategies.

Lack of social interaction: Building strong team relationships and nurturing a sense of belonging in a remote environment requires proactive efforts and dedicated initiatives.

Preparing for the Remote-First Future

Invest in technology: Implement the necessary tools and technologies to facilitate seamless remote work and collaboration.

Develop a remote-first culture: Foster a culture of trust, transparency, and inclusivity that empowers remote employees and promotes connection.

Reimagine talent acquisition: Utilize diverse recruitment channels and devise strategies to attract and retain top talent from across the globe.

Prioritize well-being: Implement initiatives that support mental and physical well-being, enabling remote employees to remain healthy and engaged.

Embrace continuous learning: Stay updated on the latest trends and technologies to thrive in the evolving landscape of remote work.

Case Study: Zapier, a prominent automation platform, is a pioneer in the remote-first world. By embracing technology, developing a strong remote culture, and prioritizing employee well-being, they have created a prospering organization.

The future of work is undeniably remote, presenting both thrilling opportunities and challenges. By embracing the potential of a global workforce and leveraging emergent technologies, businesses can flourish in this dynamic environment. By proactively addressing prospective challenges and investing in the well-being and development of their remote teams, organizations can realize the tremendous potential of the remote-first future. Remember, the key to success rests in adaptability, a commitment to continuous learning, and a proactive approach to molding the future of work for your organization and its employees.

Chapter 11: Overcoming the Challenges: Strategies for Addressing Common Remote-First Issues

While the advantages of remote-first work are compelling, certain challenges are inherent to this model. This chapter delves into the common issues encountered by remote-first businesses and equips you with practical strategies to resolve them effectively.

1. Cybersecurity Threats

Implementing robust cybersecurity measures: Utilizing secure platforms, data encryption, and strong password protocols can significantly reduce security risks.

Educating employees on cybersecurity recommended practices: Regular training sessions and awareness campaigns can help employees identify and avoid phishing attempts, malware attacks, and other hazards.

Implementing two-factor authentication (2FA): Adding a layer of security by requiring two distinct authentication factors for accessing sensitive data adds a valuable defense mechanism.

Maintaining regular backups and disaster recovery plans: Regularly storing up data and having a solid disaster recovery plan ensures business continuity in case of cyberattacks or other disruptions.

2. Time Zone Differences

Adopting asynchronous communication: Utilizing tools like project management software, email channels, and asynchronous messaging platforms allows team members to work at their tempo and collaborate effectively across different time zones.

Scheduling flexible meetings: Scheduling meetings at times that accommodate various time zones demonstrates respect for different schedules and promotes inclusivity.

Creating clear communication protocols: Establishing clear expectations for response times and availability helps ensure seamless communication and collaboration.

Leveraging technology to span the gap: Utilizing video conferencing tools with recording capabilities allows team members to partake in meetings even if they cannot attend live.

3. Managing Remote Team Dynamics

Building trust and relationships: Fostering regular communication, promoting social interaction through virtual team-building activities, and encouraging informal connections can create trust and strong relationships within the remote team.

Setting explicit expectations and goals: Establishing expectations for individual and team performance, responsibilities, and goals provides a framework for accountability and aligns everyone towards common objectives.

Providing regular feedback and recognition: Offering constructive feedback and recognizing team members' achievements motivates individuals, improves performance, and fosters a positive work environment.

Investing in training and development: Providing opportunities for skill development and career advancement demonstrates commitment to employee growth and can substantially improve retention rates.

Utilizing project management tools: Implementing collaborative project management platforms helps monitor progress, manage tasks, and facilitate communication and transparency within the team.

4. Maintaining Employee Engagement and Well-being

Promoting healthy work habits: Encouraging regular pauses, setting clear boundaries between work and personal life, and offering resources for mental health support can help prevent fatigue and promote well-being.

Creating a culture of inclusion and belonging: Fostering an environment that celebrates diversity, encourages open communication, and values individual contributions can help remote employees feel connected and engaged.

Organizing virtual social events and team-building activities: Utilizing online platforms for casual gatherings, game evenings, and social events can help create camaraderie and combat feelings of isolation.

Investing in employee well-being programs: Offering virtual fitness classes, mindfulness seminars, and access to mental health resources demonstrates a commitment to employee well-being and can substantially improve morale and engagement.

5. Measuring Success in a Remote-First Environment

Defining key performance indicators (KPIs): Identifying specific metrics aligned with your business objectives allows you to monitor progress and measure the effectiveness of your remote-first strategies.

Regularly undertaking employee surveys: Gathering feedback through surveys can provide valuable insights into employee satisfaction, engagement, and potential areas for improvement.

Utilizing data analytics tools: Leveraging data analytics tools can provide valuable insights into team productivity, communication patterns, and overall performance within the remote environment.

Focusing on outcomes over output: Shifting the focus from hours worked to measurable outcomes and attained objectives allows for greater flexibility and empowers employees to manage their work effectively.

Case Study: GitHub, a prominent code repository platform, flourishes on a remote-first culture. By instituting robust cybersecurity measures, fostering asynchronous collaboration, and prioritizing employee well-being, they have overcome common challenges and created a prospering remote-first organization.

Table of comparing Traditional Business Model & Remote-First Business Model

Feature	Traditional Business Model	Remote-First Business Model
Talent Acquisition	Limited to local talent pool	Access to a global talent pool
Cost Savings	High	Potentially

	overhead costs associated with office space, utilities, and equipment	lower overhead costs due to reduced need for office space and utilities
Employee Satisfaction & Well-being	Fixed schedules and limited flexibility can lead to work-life balance challenges	Flexibility and autonomy can lead to improved employee satisfaction and well-being
Collaboration & Communication	Easier face-to-face interaction and	Requires investment in communication technology

	collaboration	and tools and strong communicatio n practices
Team Culture & Cohesion	Easier to build a strong team culture through informal interactions and shared experiences	Requires deliberate effort to build team culture and cohesion through virtual team building activities and social events
Management & Oversight	Traditional management practices rely on direct observation	Requires a shift to trust-based management and remote

	and supervision	leadership techniques
Security & Data Privacy	Physical security measures and data security protocols are implemented within the office environment	Requires robust cybersecurity measures and data encryption protocols to protect sensitive information
Technology & Tools	Basic office equipment and software are sufficient	Requires investment in robust communication and collaboration tools, project

		management software, and security solutions
Innovation & Creativity	Face-to-face interaction and brainstorming sessions can foster creativity	Requires intentional practices to encourage collaboration and out-of-the-box thinking in a virtual environment
Scalability	Easier to scale physical operations and hire additional	Requires careful planning and consideration for time zones

employees and cultural locally differences when scaling a remote team

While challenges exist, the benefits of remote-first work outweigh them when addressed effectively. By implementing the strategies detailed in this chapter, you can navigate the common issues associated with remote work, develop a strong and connected team, and create a thriving remote-first organization that attracts and retains top talent, fosters innovation, and achieves remarkable results. Remember, the key rests in a proactive approach, continuous learning, and a commitment to establishing a positive and supportive environment for your remote team.

Chapter 12: The Remote-First Advantage: Building a Sustainable and Resilient Business

In the ever-evolving landscape of business, the remote-first model arises as a potent catalyst for growth, sustainability, and resilience. This chapter delves into the competitive advantages of embracing a remote-first approach, highlighting its impact on talent acquisition, operational efficiency, and employee engagement.

The Talent Acquisition Advantage

Access to a global talent pool: Remote work opens doors to a diverse population of experienced individuals, regardless of their location, allowing you to attract and retain top talent without geographical limitations.

Reduced recruitment costs: By eliminating geographical barriers, you can substantially reduce recruitment costs associated with travel, relocation assistance, and physical office space.

Enhanced diversity and inclusion: A remote-first workforce fosters a more diverse and inclusive workplace, promoting various perspectives, ideas, and experiences to contribute to organizational success.

The Operational Efficiency Advantage

Reduced overhead costs: Ditching the traditional office space leads to significant cost savings on rent, utilities, furniture, and other operational expenses.

Increased flexibility and scalability: A remote workforce allows you to adapt rapidly to changing market conditions and scale your operations efficiently without geographical constraints.

Improved environmental sustainability: Reduced need for tangible office space translates to less environmental impact through lower energy consumption and reduced carbon footprint.

The Employee Engagement Advantage

Improved work-life balance: Remote work offers employees greater flexibility and control over their schedules, promoting a healthy work-life balance and reducing stress levels.

Increased job satisfaction and engagement: Studies show that remote employees often experience higher levels of job satisfaction and engagement, leading to enhanced productivity and performance.

Reduced employee turnover: By offering flexible work arrangements and nurturing a positive remote culture, you can substantially reduce employee turnover and retain top talent.

Building a Sustainable and Resilient Business

Enhanced business continuity: A geographically dispersed workforce minimizes the impact of unanticipated circumstances such as natural disasters or pandemics, ensuring business continuity and operational resilience.

Improved communication and collaboration: Remote-first organizations invest in comprehensive communication tools and methodologies, leading to improved communication and collaboration across teams and locations.

Increased agility and innovation: The flexibility and diversity of a remote-first environment fosters a culture of innovation, allowing businesses to adapt to changing market trends and develop new solutions with greater agility.

Case Study: Automattic, the juggernaut behind WordPress, has successfully built a sustainable and resilient business by employing a remote-first model. Their global workforce reduced administrative costs, and focus on employee well-being have resulted in remarkable growth, financial stability, and a flourishing company culture.

The remote-first model offers a compelling path to establishing a sustainable and resilient business in today's dynamic world. By leveraging the talent acquisition advantage, operational efficiency benefits, and employee engagement advantages, you can unlock extraordinary potential for your organization. Remember, the key to success rests in embracing a strategic approach, nurturing a positive and supportive remote culture, and continuously adapting to the evolving landscape of work. By investing in your remote-first future, you can create a prospering organization that attracts and retains top talent, fosters innovation, and achieves remarkable success in the long term.

Conclusion: Embracing the Remote-First Revolution

As we close the final chapter of this voyage, let us reflect on the transformative force of the remote-first model. We have witnessed how it revolutionizes talent acquisition, uncovers operational efficiencies, and empowers employees to flourish. The statistics speak volumes: a global remote workforce exceeding 1.8 billion by 2027, a dramatic shift in employee preferences towards flexibility, and the rise of pioneering remote-first companies like Zapier and Automattic.

This book has equipped you with the knowledge and strategies to navigate this dynamic landscape. We investigated the essential elements of a scalable remote infrastructure, the art of leading geographically dispersed teams, and the significance of fostering a strong and connected remote culture. We disclosed the challenges and provided practical solutions for overcoming them, emphasizing cybersecurity, time zone differences, and managing remote team dynamics.

But the voyage doesn't end here. The remote-first revolution is just beginning, and the possibilities are endless. As you adopt this transformative model, recall these key takeaways:

• Talent knows no borders: Leverage the immense potential of a global talent pool to attract top minds regardless of their location.

• Flexibility fosters innovation: Empower your team with the freedom to work from anywhere, anytime, and unleash their maximum creative potential.

• Connection is the cornerstone: Build a vibrant remote culture that fosters trust, collaboration, and a sense of belonging, ensuring everyone feels valued and engaged.

• Continuous learning is key: Stay apprised of the latest trends and technologies in the remote-first world to adapt and flourish in the ever-evolving landscape of work.

The future of employment is undeniably remote. Will you be a protagonist in this revolution? Will you seize the opportunity to construct a sustainable, resilient, and vibrant organization that attracts and retains top talent? The choice is yours. Embrace the challenges, embrace the opportunities, and embrace the transformative force of the remote-first world. Let's embark on this voyage together and construct the future of work, one connected team at a time.

FINAL WORDS FROM THE AUTHOR

Believe in the Power of Remote-First: A Message of Inspiration and Motivation

As we stand on the precipice of a new era in the world of work, I want to share a message of optimism, encouragement, and unwavering belief in the potential of the remote-first model. This is not just a fleeting trend; it is a fundamental transformation in how we view work, talent, and the very essence of collaboration and innovation.

Imagine a world where talent knows no borders, where individuals are empowered to work from anywhere, anytime, and discharge their utmost potential. A world where organizations are dynamic and adaptable, able to respond to changing market conditions and flourish in an increasingly competitive global landscape. This is the world we are constructing, brick by brick, with every step towards a remote-first future.

The statistics are staggering. The global remote workforce is projected to reach 1.8 billion by 2027. Studies demonstrate that remote employees experience higher levels of job satisfaction and engagement, leading to enhanced productivity and performance. Companies like Automattic and Zapier are thriving evidence of the financial viability and innovation nurtured by a remote-first culture.

But let me be explicit, this voyage is not without its challenges. Time zone differences, cybersecurity threats, and managing remote team dynamics require cautious planning and proactive solutions. Yet, for every obstacle, there is a solution. We have investigated these challenges in detail throughout this book, providing you with the knowledge and strategies to navigate them effectively.

Here's what I implore you to remember:

• Believe in the power of human connection: Despite the physical distance, cultivate a vibrant remote culture that fosters trust, collaboration, and a sense of belonging. Remember, connection is the cornerstone of any successful team, regardless of location.

• Embrace continuous learning: Stay abreast of the latest trends and technologies in the remote-first world. Invest in training and development for leaders and team members to ensure everyone has the skills and knowledge to flourish in this dynamic environment.

• Lead with empathy and understanding: Recognize remote work's unique challenges and opportunities. Create a supportive environment where team members feel valued, heard, and empowered to do their best work.

• Be a champion of change: Embrace the transformative force of the remote-first model. Be a leader, an advocate, and a voice for the future of work where flexibility, inclusivity, and innovation prevail.

This is your moment to be a part of something greater than yourself. To establish a future of work that is sustainable, resilient, and empowering for all. Together, we can unleash the extraordinary potential of the remote-first world and create a workplace that works for everyone.

So, go forth, dream large, and let's build the future of labor together.